Sing a silver lining

songs to brighten your day

compiled and edited by Jane Sebba

A & C Black · London

First published 1998
A & C Black (Publishers) Ltd
35 Bedford Row London WC1R 4JH
© 1998 A & C Black (Publishers) Ltd

ISBN 0-7136-4751-5
Melody edition ISBN 0-7136-4825-2
Melody edition pack of 5 ISBN 0-7136-4827-9
Classroom edition with CD ISBN 0-7136-4824-4
Classroom edition with cassette ISBN 0-7136-4823-6

All rights reserved. No part of this publication may be reproduced or used in any form or by any means - photographic, electronic or mechanical, including photocopying, recording, taping or information storage and retrieval systems - without the prior permission in writing of the publishers.

Music setting by Andrew Jones
Cover illustration by Louise Batchelor and Sarah Godwin
Illustrations by Charlotte Hard
Design by Dorothy Moir
Edited by Jane Sebba

Printed in Great Britain by
St Edmundsbury Press Ltd,
Bury St Edmunds, Suffolk

The Sing a Silver Lining recording
Vocal lines performed by Laura Ellis and Ben Parry
Instruments performed by:
    Mark Anderson - piano
    Stan Bourke - drums
    Sandy Burnett - bass
Recording engineered by John Whiting
72 minutes playing time
All rights reserved. Copying, public performance and broadcasting - in whole or in part - of the recording are prohibited by law.

Contents

1 Sing
2 Fortuosity
3 Happy talk
4 Whistle while you work
5 Look for the silver lining
6 Silver and gold
7 We want to sing
8 On a wonderful day like today
9 You can do it
10 Zip-a-dee-doo-dah
11 Day off
12 Who will buy
13 The first time
14 The bare necessities
15 Friends
16 Consider yourself

Acknowledgements
Index of titles and first lines

Introduction

This book evolved as a result of years of tuneful singing sessions in London primary schools. I have found that children respond extremely well to 'real' songs, songs which are not 'children's songs' but which are nevertheless very appropriate to them. These songs are about friendship but don't mention love, and their sentiments are highly moral. Children are delighted when they find that their parents, sometimes even grandparents know the songs they are singing, and of course so are the grandparents! Many visitors, who came to school while these singing sessions were in progress, were amazed at the sight of eleven year old boys standing up to sing a solo. The joy of the song had overpowered all inhibitions! Some of these songs are now available under one roof, and the roof is **Sing a silver lining**.

The piano accompaniments are easy to play but, even where simplified, have not lost any of their original sparkle. You'll find the melody of the song is always there in the right hand. Some of the piano parts include small notes - these are optional extras which can be played if you wish. In some places they show syllable changes from verse to verse.

Ten of the songs include a second vocal part. These parts have been carefully written for easy learning, and yet they are melodic lines in their own right. Not only are they optional, but they can also be played on a descant recorder. Where an occasional note goes too low for the recorder, an alternative is shown.

Guitar chords are also included. The more unusual chords are shown on the first page of each song. Occasionally, if the chord in the piano part is particularly obscure, an easier alternative has been substituted for the guitar.

A recording of all the songs with separate backing tracks is available on cassette/CD. Listen to the songs, learn how both the voice parts sound, or sing along with the backing tracks.

This book is dedicated to Linda Read and all the other teachers and children who sang these songs and many more with joy and gusto.

Jane Sebba, 1998

1 · Sing

Words and music by Joe Raposo

Sing!
Sing a song.
Sing out loud, sing out strong.
Sing of good things, not bad;
Sing of happy, not sad.

Sing!
Sing a song.
Make it simple to last your whole life long.
Don't worry that it's not good enough
For anyone else to hear.
Just sing!
Sing a song!

La la la la la…

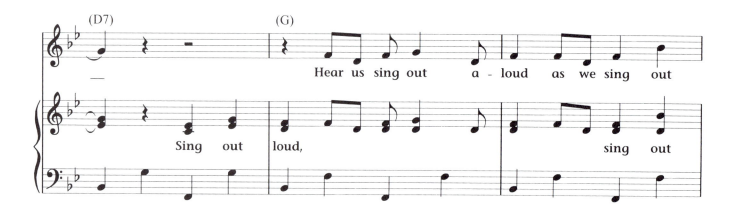

Sing

Sing

Sing

2 · Fortuosity from Walt Disney's 'The Happiest Millionaire'

Cheerful and bright

Words and music by Richard M. Sherman and Robert B. Sherman

1.
Fortuosity, that's me by word.
Fortuosity, me twinkle in the eye word.
Sometimes castles fall to the ground,
   but that's where four-leaf clovers are
      found.
Fortuosity, lucky chances.
Fortuitious little, happy happenstances.
I don't worry 'cause ev'rywhere I see that
   ev'ry bit of life is lit by
      fortuosity!

2.
Fortuosity, that's me own word.
Fortuosity, me never feel alone word.
'Round a corner, under a tree,
   good fortune's waitin', just wait and see.
Fortuosity, lucky chances.
Fortuitious little, happy happenstances.
I keep smilin', 'cause my philosophy is
'Do your best and leave the rest to
   fortuosity!'

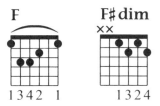

Fortuosity

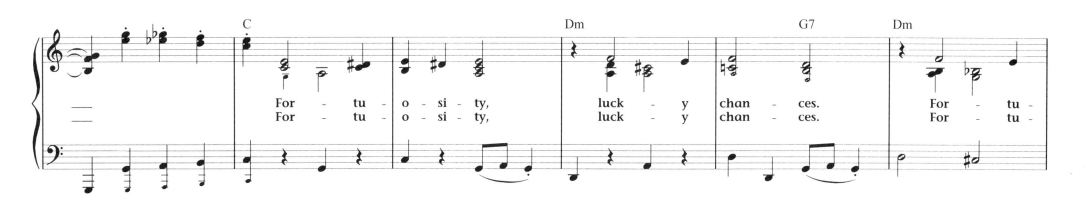

Fortuosity

3 · Happy talk

chorus
Happy talk, keep talking happy talk,
Talk about things you'd like to do.
You gotta have a dream,
If you don't have a dream
How you gonna have a dream come true?

1.
Talk about a moon,
Floating in the sky,
Looking like a lily on a lake;
Talk about a bird,
Learning how to fly,
Making all the music he can make.

chorus
Happy talk, keep talking happy talk…

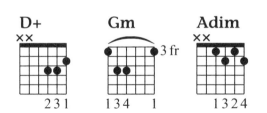

Happy talk

2.
Talk about a star,
Looking like a toy,
Peeking through the branches of a tree;
Talk about a girl,
Talk about a boy,
Counting all the ripples on the sea.

chorus
Happy talk, keep talking happy talk...

If you don't talk happy,
And you never have a dream
Then you'll never have a dream come true!

Happy talk

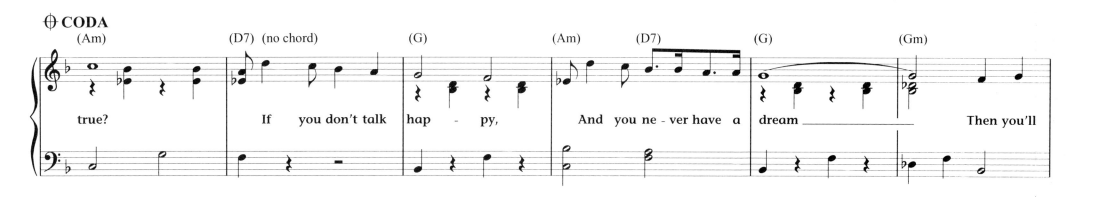
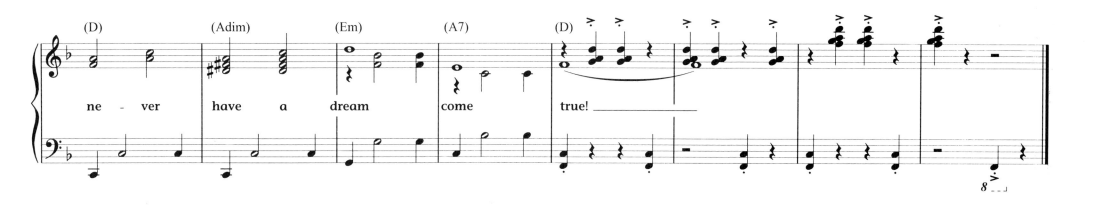

4 · Whistle while you work

Words by Larry Morey
Music by Frank Churchill

Just whistle while you work,
Put on that grin
And start right in
To whistle loud and long.

Just hum a merry tune.
Just do your best,
Then take a rest,
And sing yourself a song.

When there's too much to do,
Don't let it bother you,
Forget your trouble,
Try to be just like the cheerful chickadee,

And whistle while you work.
Come on, get smart,
Tune up and start,
To whistle while you work.

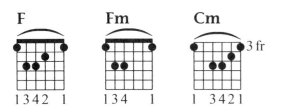

Whistle while you work

Whistle while you work

5 · Look for the silver lining

Words by Bud da Sylva
Music by Jerome Kern

Look for the silver lining,
Whene'er a cloud appears in the blue.
Remember somewhere the sun is shining,
And so the right thing to do is make it
   shine for you.

A heart full of joy and gladness
Will always banish sadness and strife.
So always look for the silver lining,
And try to find the sunny side of life!

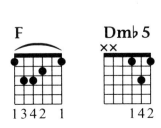

Look for the silver lining

Look for the silver lining

6 · Silver and gold

With a strong reggae beat

Words and music by Ana Sanderson

1.
You don't need a metal detector to find the
  greatest treasure,
You don't need a spade to dig deep into the
  ground,
You don't need to find a pirate's ship
  sailing across the ocean blue,
All you've got to do is open your eyes and
  look around.
Your world is full of treasures,
Your treasures are your friends;
So:

chorus
Make new friends but keep the old.
The one is silver and the other is gold.
That's the wisest thing I've been told;
Make new friends but keep the old.
The one is silver and the other is gold.

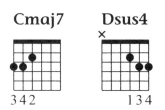

Silver and gold

2.
Sometimes friends will argue and fight
  about things which aren't important,
Sometimes friends can let you down,
  leaving you upset.
If you feel that you don't understand,
  yet you don't want to lose your friend,
All you've got to do is try to forgive and
  to forget.
Just try to make amends.
Remember they're your friends.
And

chorus
Make new friends but keep the old...

Silver and gold

(rap)
Make new friends but keep the old,
The one is silver and the other gold.
That's the wisest thing I've been told
About my silver and gold!

(sing)
Silver and gold,
My new friends and old.
They are my greatest treasure,
They are my hours of pleasure.
How sad it would be if
I never could be with
My most precious treasure,
My silver and gold.

Silver and gold,
My new friends and old...

Silver and gold

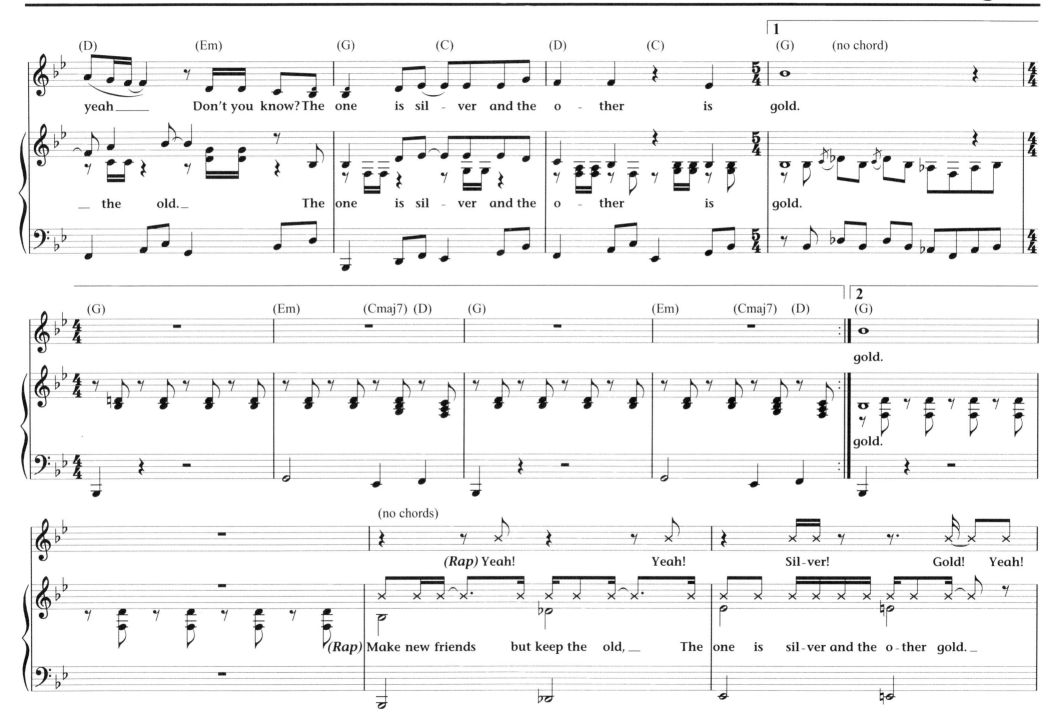

Silver and gold

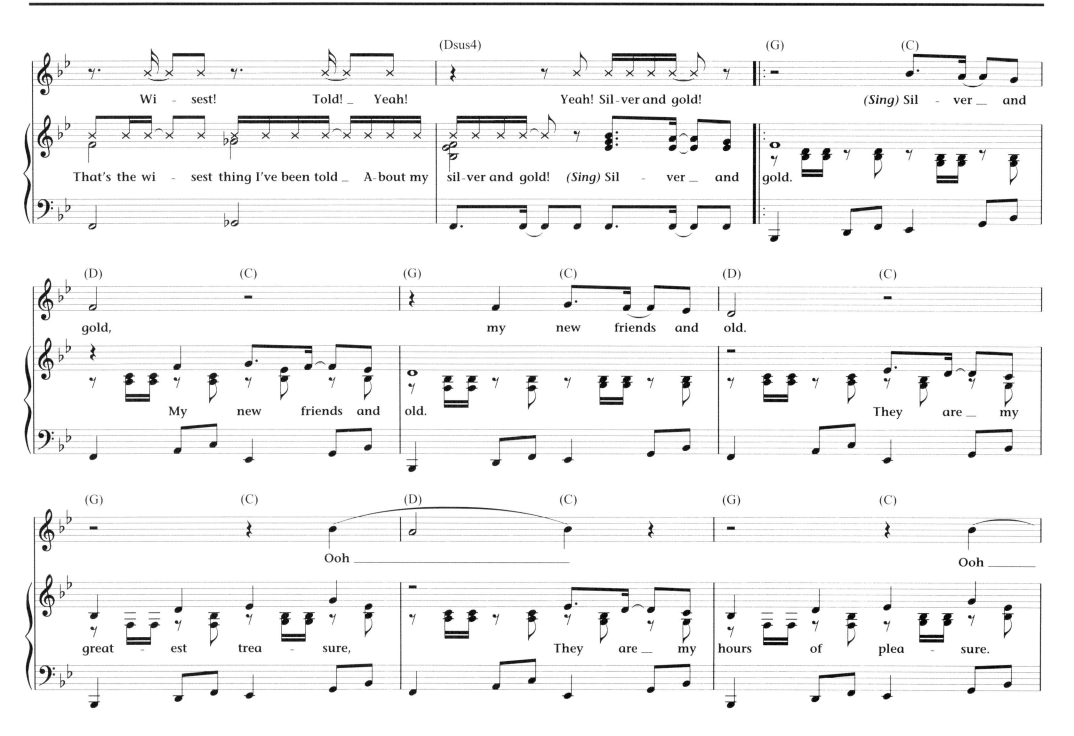

Silver and gold

7 · We want to sing

Words and music by Roger Emerson

We want to sing;
We want to tell the world;
We want them to know
That they are loved.
With our music
We can make the world a better place
For ev'ryone.

The songs that we sing have a special ring;
The people we meet can't be beat.
The days that we spend, we hope will
    never end,
So join in now, my friend.

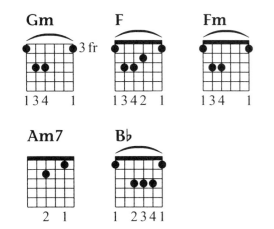

We want to sing

We want to sing;
We want to tell the world;
We want them to know
That they are loved.
With our music
We can make the world a better place
For ev'ryone.

The lives that we live have so much to give;
The love that we share soon returns.
In song and in verse our friendship we rehearse,
So join in now, my friend.

We want to sing;
We want to tell the world;
We want them to know
That they are loved.
With our music
We can make the world;
We can make the world;
We can make the world a better place
For ev'ryone.

We want to sing

We want to sing

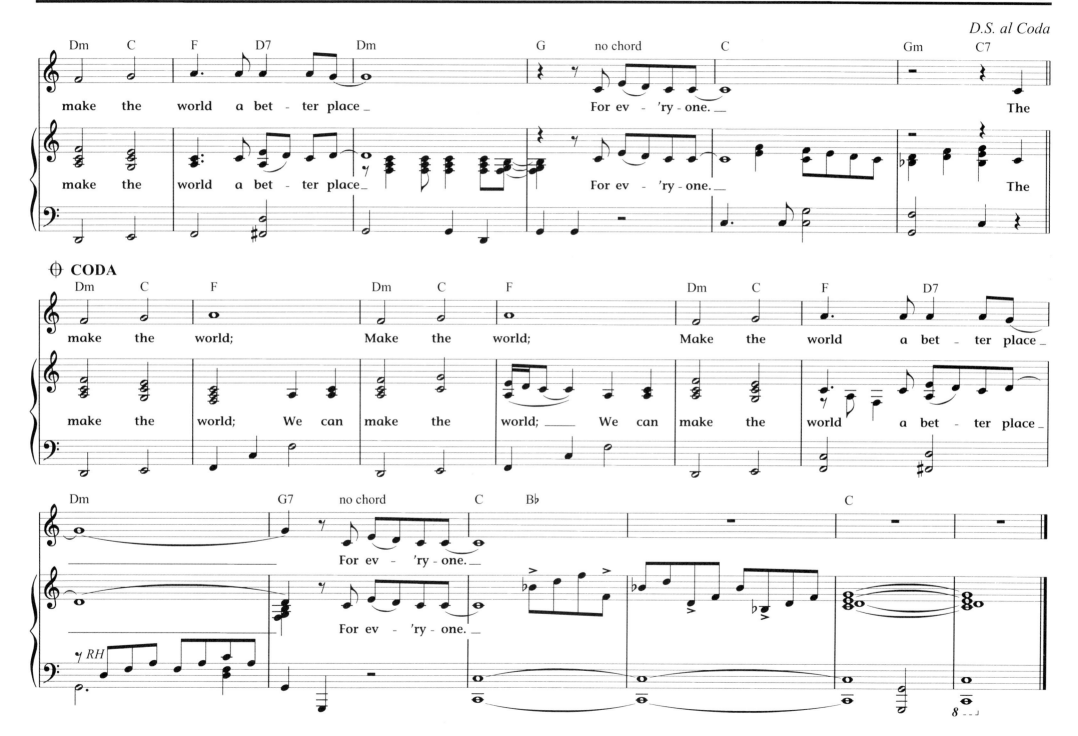

8 · On a wonderful day like today

Words and music by Leslie Bricusse and Anthony Newley

On a wonderful day like today
I defy any cloud to appear in the sky,
Dare any raindrop to plop in my eye
On a wonderful day like today.

On a wonderful morning like this
When the sun is as big as a yellow balloon,
Even the sparrows are singing in tune
On a wonderful morning like this.

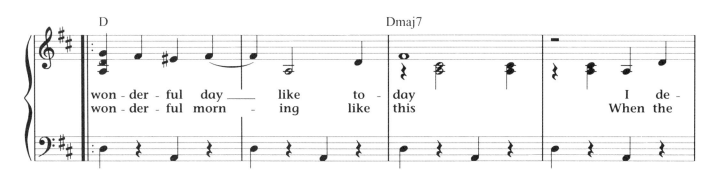

On a wonderful day like today

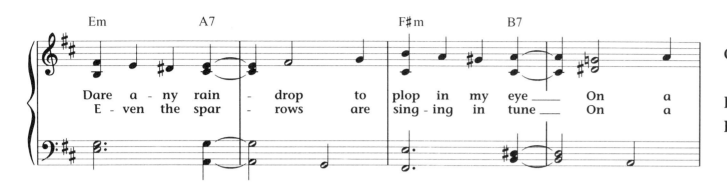

On a morning like this I could kiss
  ev'rybody,
I'm so full of love and goodwill.
Let me say furthermore I'd adore
  ev'rybody to come and dine,
  The pleasure's mine,
  And I will pay the bill.

May I take this occasion to say
That the whole human race should go
  down on its knees,
Show that we're grateful for mornings like
  these,
For the world's in a wonderful way,
On a wonderful day like today.

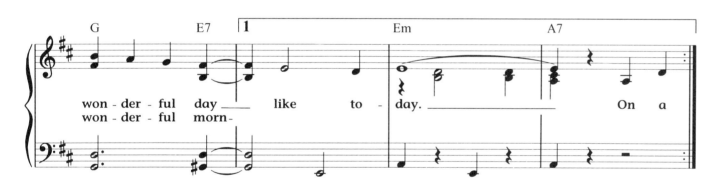

On a wonderful day like today

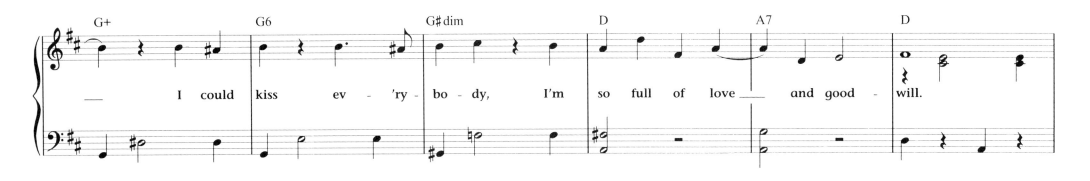

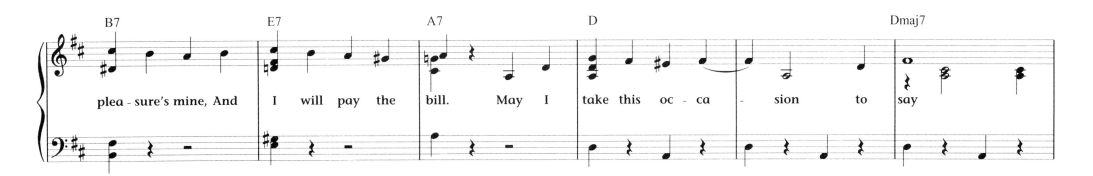

On a wonderful day like today

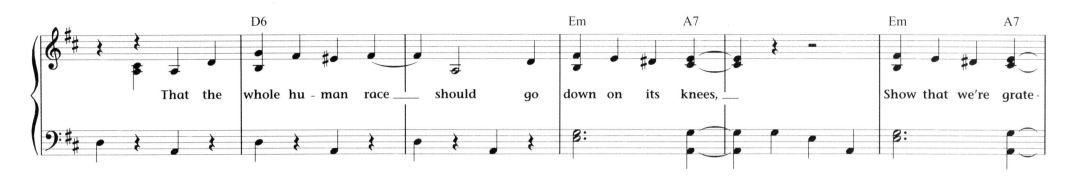

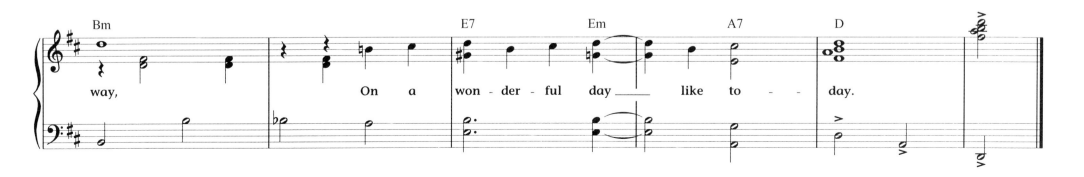

9 · You can do it

Words and music by Jane Sebba

chorus

You can do it,

You can do it,

You can do it if you really try.

    You can meet that challenge,

    Beat that challenge,

    If you really try,

And when you've succeeded you'll feel

    Nine feet high.

1.

Sums are hard with all that dividing,

Adding makes me feel like hiding,

I just want to take it all away.

    Multiplying's even worse,

    It makes me want to scream and curse,

    But then I hear a little voice inside me

    say:

chorus

You can do it…

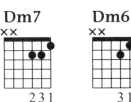
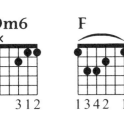
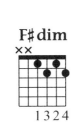

You can do it

3.
When I'm swimming deep in the water,
Even though I know I ought to
Kick my legs, that sinking feeling's there.
    Then I feel my head go under,
    That's when I begin to wonder
    If I'll hear a little voice in me declare:

You can do it,
You can do it,
You can do it if you really try.
    You can meet that challenge,
    Beat that challenge,
    If you really try,
And when you've completed it,
Defeated and repeated it,
You'll feel so high you'll want to touch
    the sky.

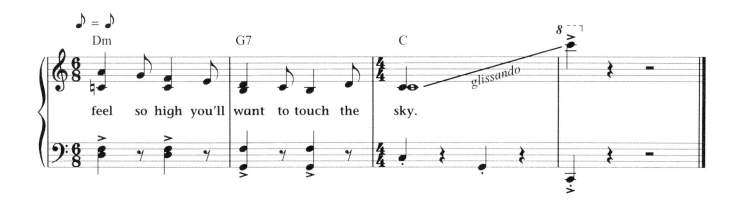

10 · *Zip-a-dee-doo-dah*

Words by Ray Gilbert
Music by Allie Wrubel

Cheerfully

This is just the kind of day that you dream about,

When you open up your mouth a song pops out.

Zip-a-dee-doo-dah,

Zip-a-dee-ay,

My, oh my, what a wonderful day!

Plenty of sunshine heading my way,

Zip-a-dee-doo-dah,

Zip-a-dee-ay!

Mister Bluebird on my shoulder,

It's the truth, it's 'act-ch'll',

Ev'rything is 'satisfact-ch'll',

Zip-a-dee-doo-dah,

Zip-a-dee-ay!

Wonderful feeling,

Wonderful day.

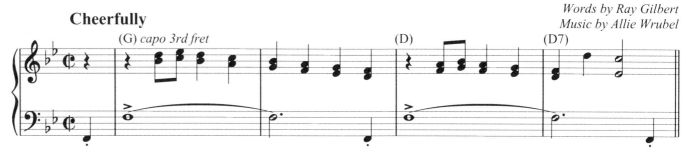

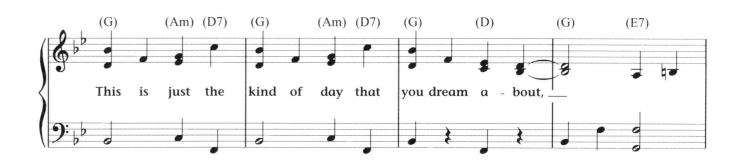

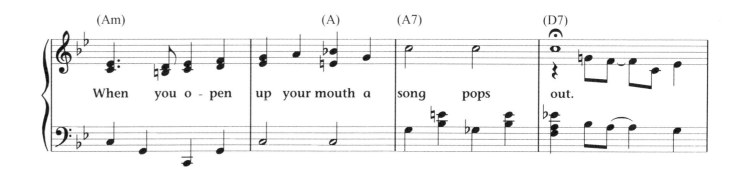

Zip-a-dee-doo-dah

Zip-a-dee-doo-dah

11 · Day off

Words and music by Malcolm Abbs

chorus
I've got a day off,
I know just where I'll be,
I've got a day off,
I know just what to see,
I've got a day off
To take a trip or two round the world.

1.
I'll watch the sun rise on the Great Wall of
    China,
Play with a porpoise in the Caspian Sea,
I'm going to go to Nepal and climb a
    mountain that's tall
And drop into Darjeeling for tea.
I'll join a mariachi band in Mexico,
I'll write my name in soft Sahara sand,
I'll eat a biscuit in Nice and count the
    islands of Greece
And yodelay in Switzerland.

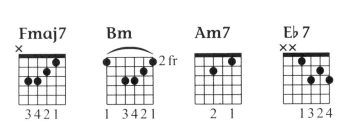

Day off

chorus
I've got a day off...

2.
I'll take a long cool drink in Zanzibar,
I'll play a mean kazoo in Kalamazoo,
I'll ride a hot air balloon from Dunoon to Kowloon
And walk from Chile up to Peru.
I'll wear a straw hat on the streets of Panama,
Run up and down the Russian Steppes for fun,
I'll dance the limbo in style around a tropical isle,
In Sweden see the midnight sun.

Day off

chorus

I've got a day off...

I've got a day off
To take a trip or two round the world.
I've got a day off
To take a trip or two round the world.

por - poise in the Cas - pi - an Sea, ___ I'm going to
mean ka - zoo in Ka - la - ma - zoo, ___ I'll ride a

go to Ne - pal __ and climb a moun - tain that's tall __ And
hot air bal - loon __ from Du - noon __ to Kow - loon __ And

drop in - to Dar - jee - ling for tea. ___ I'll join a
walk from Chi - le up to Pe - ru. ___ I'll wear a

ma - ri - a - chi band in Mex - i - co, ___ I'll write my
straw hat on the streets of Pa - na - ma, __ Run up and

Day off

12 · Who will buy

Words and music by Lionel Bart

Brightly

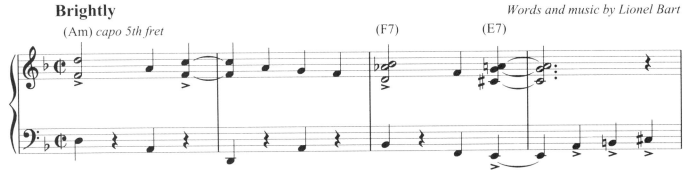

Who will buy this wonderful morning?
Such a sky you never did see!
Who will tie it up with a ribbon,
And put it in a box for me?
   So I can see it at my leisure,
     Whenever things go wrong,
      And I would keep it as a treasure
     To last my whole life long!
Who will buy this wonderful feeling?
I'm so high, I swear I could fly.
Me, oh my, I don't want to lose it,
So what am I to do
To keep the sky so blue?
There must be someone who will buy.

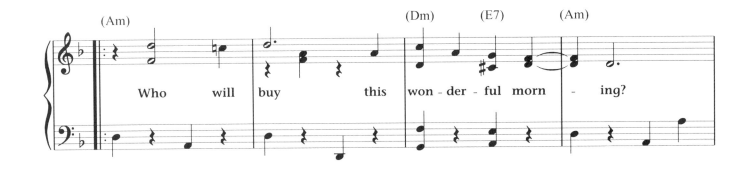

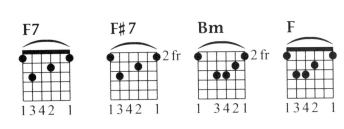

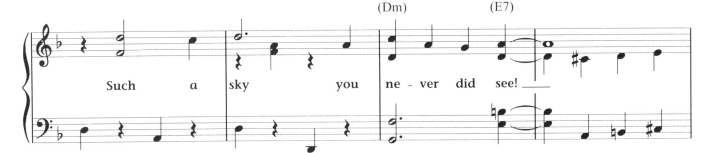

Who will buy

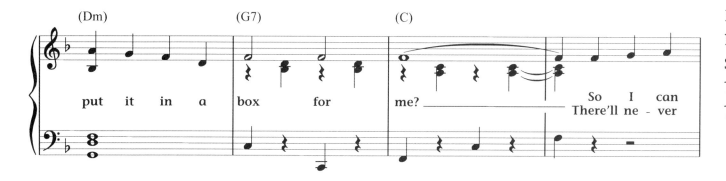

Who will buy this wonderful morning?
Such a sky you never did see!
Who will tie it up with a ribbon,
And put it in a box for me?
    There'll never be a day so sunny,
    It could not happen twice.
    Where is the man with all the money?
    It's cheap at half the price!
Who will buy this wonderful feeling?
I'm so high, I swear I could fly.
Me, oh my, I don't want to lose it,
So what am I to do
To keep the sky so blue?
There must be someone who will buy.

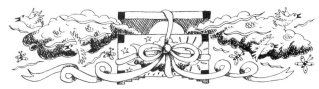

Who will buy

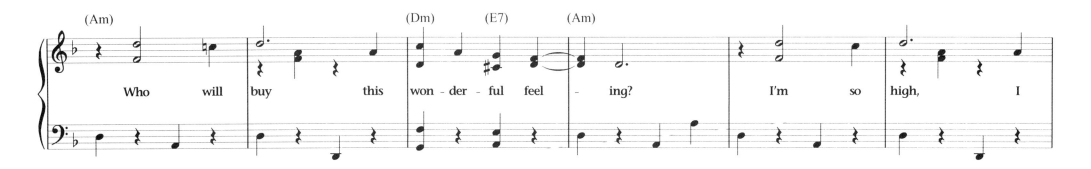

Who will buy

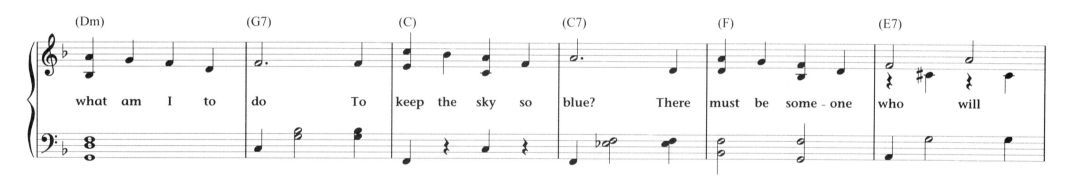
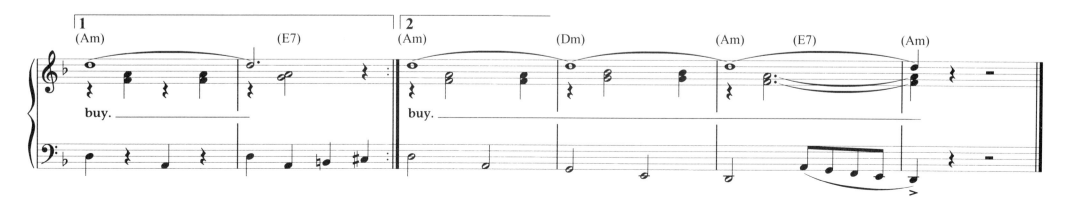

13 · The first time

Words and music by Tony Geiss

It's harder, the first time,
The first time you try.
It's crazy, that first time,
You're scared and you're shy.
You're feeling that feeling
Of starting to do
Something that's strange and new.

That first time's the tough time;
You try and you try.
It's trouble, big trouble,
You may have to cry.
You get it! You lose it!
You fall down and then you
Pick yourself up and try again.

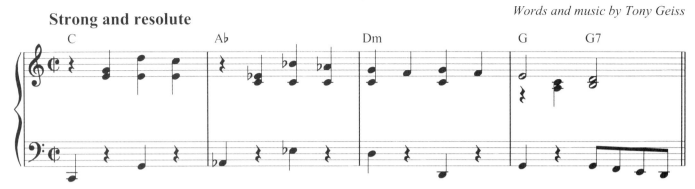

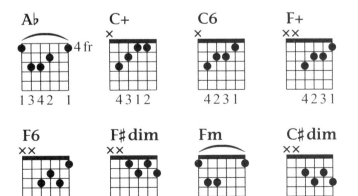

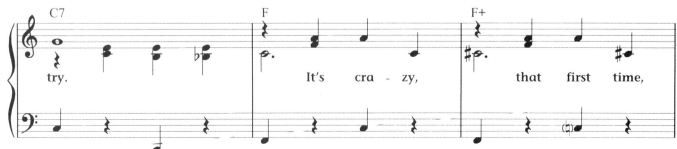

The first time

You're working! You're striving!
You're struggling now.
Then all of a sudden,
All of a sudden,
All of a sudden you know how!

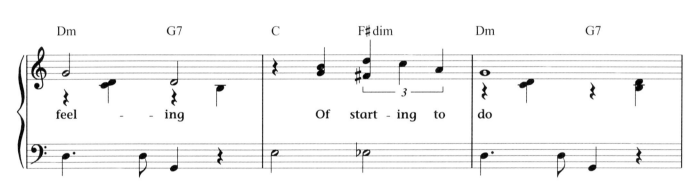

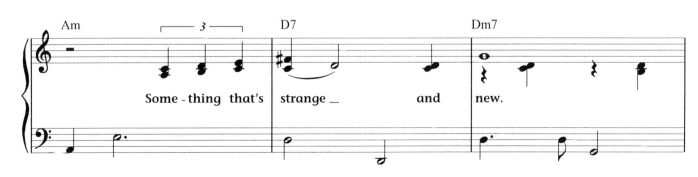

The first time

The first time

14 · The Bare Necessities from Walt Disney's 'The Jungle Book'

Words and music by Terry Gilkyson

Bright and with spirit

1.
Look for the bare necessities,
   the simple bare necessities;
   forget about your worries and
   your strife.
I mean the bare necessities,
Or Mother Nature's recipes
   that bring the bare necessities of life.

Wherever I wander, wherever I roam,
I couldn't be fonder of my big home.
The bees are buzzin' in the tree
   to make some honey just for me.
You look under the rocks and plants and
   take a glance at the fancy ants,
   then maybe try a few.
The bare necessities of life will come
   to you,
   they'll come to you!

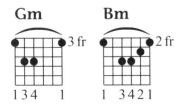

The bare necessities

2.

Look for the bare necessities,
   the simple bare necessities;
   forget about your worries and your strife.
I mean the bare necessities,
That's why a bear can rest at ease
   with just the bare necessities of life.

When you pick a paw-paw or prickly pear,
   and you prick a raw paw next time
beware.
Don't pick the prickly pear by paw,
   when you pick a pear, try to use the claw.
But you don't need to use the claw
   when you
Pick a pear of the big paw-paw,
   have I given you a clue?
The bare necessities of life will come to
you,
   they'll come to you!

The bare necessities

3.
Look for the bare necessities,
    the simple bare necessities;
        forget about your worries and your strife.
I mean the bare necessities,
Or Mother Nature's recipes
    that bring the bare necessities of life.

So just try to relax (Oh yeah!) in my
    back yard,
        if you act like that bee acts you're
        workin' too hard.
Don't spend your time just lookin' around
    for something you want that can't
    be found.
When you find out you can live without
    it and
    go along not thinkin' about it.
I'll tell you something true.
The bare necessities of life will come to you,
    they'll come to you!

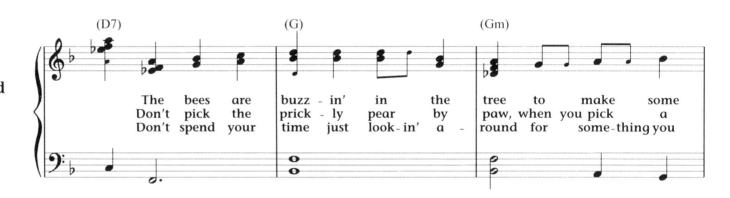

The bare necessities

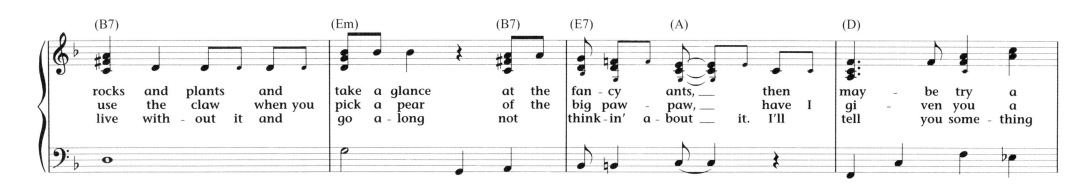
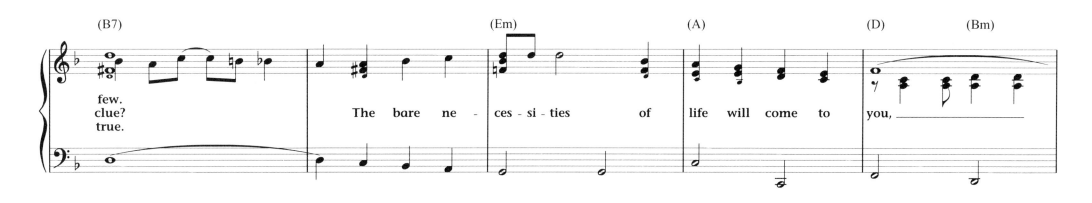
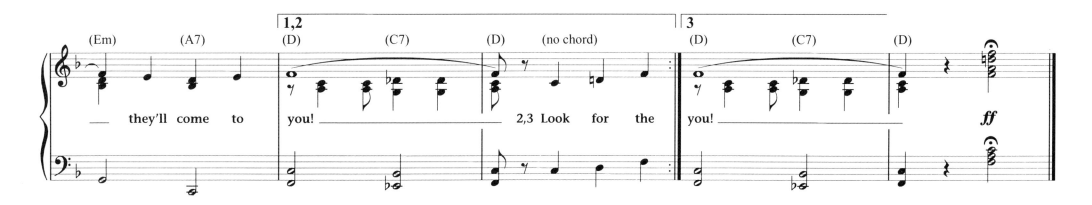

15 · Friends

Words by David Croft
Music by Cyril Ornadel

Friends,
Isn't it rather nice to have
Friends,
Isn't it rather nice to have
Friends to rely upon,
Shoulders to cry upon,
You must have friends.

Friends,
How can you get along without
Friends,
How can you get along without
Someone to help you out,
When you are down and out,
You must have friends.

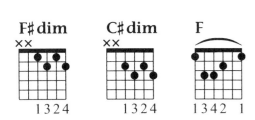

Friends

I rely on my friends,
They help me in all I do.
I don't try to buy friends,
For though it seems funny,
No amount of money buys

Friends,
Nothing is quite complete without
Friends,
And if you ever meet the one
Who will be part of life,
Right from the start of life,
Until the end,
Then, my friend, you've made a friend.

Friends

Friends

16 · Consider yourself

Words and music by Lionel Bart

1.
Consider yourself at home,
Consider yourself one of the family,
We've taken to you so strong
It's clear we're going to get along!
Consider yourself well in,
Consider yourself part of the furniture,
There isn't a lot to spare;
Who cares? Whatever we've got, we share!
   If it should chance to be we should see
      some harder days,
   Empty larder days, why grouse?
   Always a chance we'll meet somebody to
      foot the bill,
   Then the drinks are on the house!
Consider yourself our mate,
We don't want to have no fuss
For after some consideration we can state:
Consider yourself one of us.

Consider yourself

2.
Consider yourself at home,
Consider yourself one of the family,
We've taken to you so strong
It's clear we're going to get along!
Consider yourself well in,
Consider yourself part of the furniture,
There isn't a lot to spare;
Who cares? Whatever we've got we share!
> Nobody tries to be lah-di-dah and uppity,
> There's a cup o' tea for all.
> Only it's wise to be handy wiv a rolling pin,
> When the landlord comes to call!

Consider yourself our mate,
We don't want to have no fuss
For after some consideration we can state:
Consider yourself one of us.

Consider yourself

Consider yourself

Acknowledgements

We are grateful to the following copyright owners who have kindly granted their permission for the inclusion of these items:

Consider yourself words and music by Lionel Bart. © 1959 LAKEVIEW MUSIC PUBLISHING CO. LTD. of Suite 2.07, Plaza 535 Kings Road, London SW10 0SZ. International Copyright Secured. All Rights Reserved. Used by Permission.

Day off words and music by Malcolm Abbs. © 1997 Malcolm Abbs, A&C Black (Publishers) Ltd.

Fortuosity words and music by Richard M Sherman, Robert B Sherman. Copyright © 1966 by Wonderland Music Company Inc. Campbell Connelly & Co Ltd., 8/9 Frith St., London W1V 5TZ. International Copyright Secured. All Rights Reserved.

Friends words by David Croft, music by Cyril Ornadel. © 1997 Chappell Music Limited, London W1Y 3FA. Reproduced by permission of International Music Publications Ltd.

Happy talk words by Oscar Hammerstein II, music by Richard Rodgers. Copyright © 1949 by Richard Rodgers and Oscar Hammerstein II. Copyright Renewed. This arrangement Copyright © 1997 by WILLIAMSON MUSIC. WILLIAMSON MUSIC owner of publication and allied rights throughout the world. International Copyright Secured. All Rights Reserved.

Look for the silver lining words by Buddy De Sylva, music by Jerome Kern. © 1920 TB Harms Inc. PolyGram Music Publishing Ltd / Redwood Music Ltd, London NW1 8BD. Reproduced by permission of Music Sales Ltd. and International Music Publications Ltd.

On a wonderful day like today words and music by Leslie Bricusse and Anthony Newley. © 1964 CONCORD MUSIC LTD. of Suite 2.07, Plaza 535 Kings Road, London SW10 0SZ. International Copyright Secured. All Rights Reserved. Used by Permission.

Silver and gold words and music by Ana Sanderson. © 1997 Ana Sanderson, A&C Black (Publishers) Ltd.

Sing words and music by Joe Raposo. © 1972 Standard Music Ltd. Onward House, 11 Uxbridge Street, London W8 7TQ. © 1971 JONICO MUSIC, INC. All Rights Reserved. Used by Permission WARNER BROS. PUBLICATIONS U.S. INC., Miami, FL, 33014

The bare necessities words and music Terry Gilkyson. Copyright © 1964 by Wonderland Music Company Inc. Campbell Connelly & Co Ltd., 8/9 Frith St., London W1V 5TZ. International Copyright Secured. All Rights Reserved.

The first time words and music by Tony Geiss. © copyright 1993 Sesame Street Incorporated, The Ephemeral Music Company, Sony/ATV Tunes LLC & Sony Music International, USA. Sony/ATV Music Publishing, 10 Great Marlborough Street, London WC1. Used by permission of Music Sales Limited. All Rights Reserved, International Copyright Secured.

We want to sing words and music by Roger Emerson. Copyright © 1977 EMERSONGS. This arrangement copyright 1997 EMERSONGS. International Copyright Secured. All Rights Reserved.

Whistle while you work words by Larry Morey, music by Frank Churchill. © Copyright 1937 by Bourne Co. Copyright renewed. This Arrangement © Copyright 1997 by Bourne Co. All Rights Reserved. International Copyright Secured.

Who will buy words and music by Lionel Bart. © 1959 LAKEVIEW MUSIC PUBLISHING CO. LTD. of Suite 2.07, Plaza 535 Kings Road, London SW10 0SZ. International Copyright Secured. All Rights Reserved. Used by Permission.

You can do it words and music by Jane Sebba. © 1984 Jane Sebba. Printed by permission of Faber Music Limited, London.

Zip-a-dee-doo-dah words by Ray Gilbert, music by Allie Wrubel. © 1946, Santly-Joy Inc, USA. Reproduced by permission of EMI Music Publishing Ltd, London WC2H 0EA. © 1946 J. Albert & Son Pty Ltd for Australia & New Zealand & Walt Disney Music Company.

Every effort has been made to trace and acknowledge copyright owners. If any right has been omitted, the publishers offer their apologies and will rectify this in subsequent editions following notification.

All arrangements written by Jane Sebba, except for Day off by Malcolm Abbs, Silver and gold and The first time by Ana Sanderson, Fortuosity by Richard M. Sherman and Robert B. Sherman, and The bare necessities by Terry Gilkyson.

The compiler and publishers would also like to thank the following people who have generously assisted in the preparation of this book: Jenny Craigen, Caroline Heslop, Dorothy Moir, Sheena Roberts, Ana Sanderson, and in the preparation of the recording: Mark Anderson, Stan Bourke, Sandy Burnett, Laura Ellis, Ben Parry, and John Whiting.